# Predatory

**Pitt Poetry Series**

Ed Ochester, Editor

# Predatory

Glenn Shaheen

University of Pittsburgh Press

Published by the University of Pittsburgh Press, Pittsburgh, PA 15260
Copyright © 2011, Glenn Shaheen
All rights reserved
Manufactured in the United States of America
Printed on acid-free paper
10 9 8 7 6 5 4 3 2 1

ISBN 13: 978-0-8229-6162-8
ISBN 10: 0-8229-6162-8

# Contents

# Predatory

## Feral Cats

*could be something + cle* (handwritten, left margin)

All night, a howl
outside the window. All night an animal
is sick. I won't get any of this right
the first time.

          In Switzerland,
scientists have found the region of the brain that tricks us
into seeing ghosts. Some cloud of current
that drifts from front
of skull to back. They can fake
an out-of-body experience
by shocking the corpus callosum. A door

*So ghosts aren't real?* (handwritten, right margin)

slams shut. Now there's death
in every shadow. It's a seven-ten split. There is no wall
to shoulder up against this new logic.

Before, I thought
if it was raining here, it was raining two blocks away. The animals

are still dying. I can hear them all night. We had hoped
for the burning ghost ship of legend to light
our harbor, in front of news cameras, in front of hundreds
of witnesses. We would cheer
it home to dock. Relief. An uneasy audience
ready to laugh. The first time. A stone

*they WANT this ghost ship to come* (handwritten, right margin)

1

is tied to a hungry animal's neck. It is dropped
into a mile-deep oceanic crevice off the Aleutian Islands.
Irreversible. It takes thirty minutes
for the animal to even hit the bottom.

# Killing Machine

In the summer here it feels as though we haven't felt
the wind in ages. There is a hum
                on the air. Everybody is <u>caterwaul</u>

and jostled nerves. All picked and thrown. City officials
have <u>decided</u> on rolling blackouts. There isn't enough time to read
today's newspaper. There'll be <u>another one</u> tomorrow.

*that's different but might as well be the same.*

More and more people ask me what
        exactly I am. My flexible pallor.

I tell them I want somebody to love. I need somebody to love.

*Jefferson Airplane?*

But that's not enough.

My friend needs help
          but I don't want to help. I want to stay home
      and watch a DVD alone. Preferably a comedy

without political undertones. I am aimless. I need

a specific calendar filled with appointments. I can't even
          put my groceries away in order. I never eat
     them. They expire. They were right all along, to bring us all into

this fresh mayhem, to take down our buildings. Shaheen
means "eagle" in Arabic. I wouldn't vote if I could
*very american*

3

and this is not irresponsible. I was born in a foreign city rebuilt
from its own rubble. I know and love that the thing we all have

in common is that we are part of a great and unstoppable killing machine.

We are sure we have been the best we could have ever been.

## Dementia Unit

One moment. I remember a ditch. A ditch
where the young mother's body was
dumped. There were crosses and bluebonnets. There is

an apartment overlooking a rainy city and the news
discusses the implication of sunshine. I shake just
thinking of the airline. A company is almost

a living thing. I've forgotten who I am a few times.
From surgery, from drugs. The police are searching
all the cars on the north side of the block today,

and the south side of the block tomorrow. They say
it's very important, but I don't think there's anything
I want them to find, personally. Personally, I'd take

the door with the tiger, but that would be an accident.
It's my luck. There's a tiger behind every door. A plane
crash beneath every plane. A carjacking on every corner.

Dread sprouting from every word. From Aryan to Zion.
From Assisted Suicide to Zen Meditation. Ha! You thought
I was beyond that. Above that. A stray bullet hits

the woman in front of us at the bank. In front of both
of us. When I tell the story I say she was in front of me,
when you tell the story you say she was in front of you.

The truth is she was just in front of the bullet. What will it take for us to learn the value of our pitiful lives? I mean all of them, put together, a wisp in the corner

of a dark room, a missed word in the middle of an epic bildungsroman about sorcery and betrayal in the most carnal sense. One gasp in a silent crowd.

## New Model Honeybee

There's nothing you can do to stop it. A wind moves
over your ear, muffling
the music you thought you could hear from a car
parked outside, invisible, behind the next house. Microchip stocks

have risen dramatically in the past few weeks. Honey
is down. Honey is always down. The best men
are working on a solution. You can't
do anything except watch
the TV special on the dogface boy.
The historical dogface boy. See how they all said
he was really a genius under
all that fur? I mean, I don't want

to tell you what to do. But your worry is beginning
to seep. It's flooding the local streets. The interstates
are down to one lane. It's not
just your worry. It's becoming a pandemic. New laws

have dimmed home light bulbs. New laws forbid
the sale of baklava under all
but the most dire circumstances. New laws require the donation
of Saran Wrap to local scientific research stations.

When are you going to move closer on the couch? We don't
have all night. You told me to wash
my bedclothes and I did. You told me

to get my affairs in order. What was the first sign? What

is this humming that washes my head like a wave?
O Europe! O ton of honey! A wind

moves through your emptied ribs. The ship's fire
is put out by the water rushing into the hold.

# Introducing Love into the Fragile Texas Ecosystem

I was told it was impossible to try to be erotic
these days. People just keep thinking about suffering.
The real kind
and the kind written into shows about men with guns
and impeccable aim. Who can get off in that kind of mood,

anyway? Hey, I didn't start this show trial.
Just the other day here
a middle-school student was expelled for licking his girlfriend's
face in science class.
Now he's a junior hero.

None of the other kids are even brave enough to brush
against each other gently on the bus. They speak
of him in hushed tones. Like John Henry. Roswell.
Any great American myth. And us adults?

Something cracked
the ground. We've been sucked
into the latest story in the great saga of fire. There are hundreds
of drugs designed to cater to all

our erectile needs. But heat?
Sapped. Baby, I'd like to tell you
how I would cup your breast. Your naked breast. Cup it

in my hand and let the nipple slide between

my fingers. This is what I'd like
to tell you. With the greatest confidence
and ease. I'd like to say we could coil into each other

like a Pfizer truck T-boning a gasoline truck
in rush-hour traffic. The names of the dead aren't
what people would remember about that, you know.

## Longest Day of the Year

Now there is one less person who loves you in the world.

A scratching in the wall when you try to sleep.

When a plant in the nature video brushes gently against another on wind you mistake it for real human emotion.

From here things only get worse. Your friends divorce. Your family dies. Disease. Crumbling ground over a deep chasm. You aren't able to run anymore.

There are those who still believe in the ultimate power of the lightbulb over sun. There are those who still believe in Christmas miracles. Bank errors in your favor. A mistaken notice of death. Sudden reversals. Celebrations.

In the forties, millions of dollars were sunk into a program that could make a destroyer vanish before our eyes. Ultimately it was a failure.

Love as shield. Love as cracking armor. Love as crack legal defense squad that blocks court-ordered injunctions and seizures for you by using the most arcane and hidden laws still on the books. Love as thin blanket.

Driving up the street, the incline gives you vertigo. You're certain if you looked out through the back window you would start to slide backward and not even the emergency brake could stop you.

Sun too early. Dusk too late. The rare lunar eclipse turns the moon dark red.

What tendrils could you have placed? What tendrils have you refused?

The animals smell blood and they go crazy. If its belly is empty, even the robin will feast on blood. Even the timid mealworm is vicious to dying skin.

*And love? Love will tear us apart, again.*

# A Guarantee of Protection

I, nameable. I, a collection of syllables. I, policier. I, "All
Night Long" by Lionel Richie. I, lion. I, impervious
to most insults yet few objects. I, terror incarnate. I, devil's
advocate. I, devil. I, many ones and zeros. I, proud Canadian.
I, born from ruin. I, protector of small rodents. I, filled
with bones and blood. I, mud. I, sheet music. I, broken chair.
I, unfilled calendar. I, loud music, yet played
softly. I, aimless clicking through many pages. I, summing
it all up in too few words, it gets confusing. It is called
meandering and pointless, and the important issues are lost
in the fury of it. I, unproud Arab. I, the fury of it. I, a deliveryman
of pain. Don't worry though, it's only mine. I, terrified incarnate.
I, technology. I, your voice as you hear it when you read silently.
I, silent. I, consumer watchdog on the take. I, not making it.
I, swindler. I, geekgasm. I, speechless for a change, are you
happy? I, last word, but not a very good one. Tell them I said
something. I, the filth and the shit. I, an impenetrable shield.
I, happy for a bit. Come to me if you want to know the truth
about me. I, a little bit of truth here and there. I, the fox
but not the hare. I, broken down when you can't see. I,
the moment before sex, and the moment right after. I, after.
I, all night. I, misdirection incarnate, you don't know just
what it means. I, all night. I, too drunk to dance. I, all night.

## Space Phenomenon

In an episode of *Star Trek*, Dr. Crusher is trapped
in a shrinking universe, people vanishing, until she
is the only person left on board the USS *Enterprise*.
A priest assured me that in Heaven we won't worry
about our loved ones burning in Hell, because our
memory will be wiped clean of them. This love

is what we are offered by God: to forget their absence,
our brains shaken out of the last dark dregs of friends
and family. How the world. What world. I just can't
believe in anything but me. I can't picture us being
anything but a phenomenon in space. Nobody
sorts out the terrible sin from the terrible sinner.

I just want to be noticed against the backdrop. I only
want to be crowned the next Great American
Mop Bucket. Where do you fit into any of this,
you shell? You shill. In Houston, a tan haze hangs
over the city and makes the buildings look like sticks
propped against a dull curtain. In photos, Earth

is an iris drowned in pupil. A crushing black. The
unfurling of a deep fog. There's something formal
about the muzzle of a gun, I've always said, having
never held one. There is a kind of happiness out
there that each of us could probably possess,
but at what price kingdom? At what price come?

# The SS *American Star*

Somewhere a house in which a thousand dreams
were born burns to the ground. The family is inside
and dies. Or they're away
at dinner, returning to embers. The point is, many
of those dreams involved this house, its rooms, all the love
that could flood its halls. Now,
ash. Actually, we should start

smaller. Somewhere a tree house in which ten dreams
were born burns to the ground.

                    Or a woman enters a room
in the middle of a lecture and everybody turns
to see her, expecting to be astonished. A sea of heads
in one smooth wave.

But she is nobody special. She has recently
had her heart broken. Who hasn't? This is not
glamorous.
                    Years ago, the SS *American Star*

was one of the premiere cruise ships in the world.
Thousands of people rode her all over the Atlantic,
the Pacific. Celebrities. Lottery winners.

Couples blowing some of their savings. Their love
in winded tatters. Or newlyweds. Their lives

smooth glass. And singles. There was much sex and dance.
Many hoped to book

a room on the ship one day. But the ship fell apart. Bit by bit. The paint
went, and pipes. The bones couldn't hold
the skin. Passengers stopped. The ship began to haul cold

freight. Metals. Oil. Eventually, a storm wrecked
the ship at Fuerteventura, off the coast of Africa,
in shallow waters. It broke in half, two hundred yards
from shore. And it still sits, rusted, gutted of former thoughts
and the buzz of ghosts, just
offshore. The townspeople ignore it. In Arkansas,

a high school social studies teacher explains to her students that everything
they adore in life has been earned by military

action. Some amount of flame and metal has bought
all the knickknacks and meals they need

for everyday living. They realize
that this is a source for intense pride. All thirty kids breathe in
at once. This creates the smallest fluctuation
in the pressure of the classroom
killing millions of tiny germs and bacteria all housed
in the hot crevices
of their skin, invisible to the naked eye.

## Moderate Division Techniques

Just tell me how to function. How do any of us function
when we don't know where our next meal will come
from? Not that it's even remotely possible that we won't

have a next meal, but we're concerned about palatability.
We're Americans. We have the right to refuse bland meat.
That's gracious of you, yes, but there's a certain degree

of luxury we won't even admit possessing. If we miss
one episode, it's curtains. Somebody is getting maimed.
Where do I stand. A twig in the dust devil. Batted around

and mixed with all the other junk. A blustered vagrant
who stumbled into the wrong alley, beneath the buildings set
for demolition. Let's all look for a photogenic sunrise.

Break. Let's all look for a photogenic anything. Let's all
look for the photogenic picture of the child holding his
mother's arm newly shorn from its socket. That's the one

that's Pulitzer material, yes. Real blood, real suffering.
Even I know the solution is perhaps tomorrow, was yesterday,
or any day but today. We missed it in all the commotion.

Our names mumbled in the crowded bar. We think it was
just a trick of the ear, but in reality somebody was desperate
for our attention. Desperate for our voice against their own.

## Predatory

I know how to sleep next to a woman
without touching her. All the bells ringing. The A/C brushing
every hair on my body. What moves us

anyway?
            Before a car wreck, everything
seems to slow down. If you fall off a ladder, you feel
like you should hit the ground five times
before you actually do. Getting a tattoo hurts

just as much as you'd think.
                        Come on, let's all reminisce
about September 11 again. Where we were, what we were doing, what
    kind of clothes we had on. Me,
                        I was sleeping in. I was heartbroken.
                        I was living in a studio

apartment with one cat and a lot of cockroaches. These
are the kind of riveting details I can give you.
                        The countdown

has begun. The gears have been shoved
into motion. Outside, the flag is raised
                    on the tallest pole, but it is in

the lowest valley in town.
Take what you can get.

The bell struck silent, the bell struck ringing. I know a lot

of ways to sleep next to a woman. Some without
touching her.

Some predatory. Some unorthodox. I've had a lot

of secrets breathed over my ears. There's a heart
in every home. A scent in every jungle.

# The Page on which the Spine Is Broken

As though there were an interruption. A great
many things were placed on the book,
flattening it. What is on the page
doesn't matter. We may be on a road

with no turns. We may be
the ones who threw the bodies
in the reservoir, in front of

a great many witnesses. In Bodie,
California, a famous ghost town, dinner plates

are set up in the homes
as though the residents vanished
suddenly. Some murderous wind cut through
their chests one evening. Or they all crawled to the desert,
the air newly poison, each breath

a claw grasping for a ledge, any ledge. Or hands
reached from the floors and pulled them through.

A cyclone is on the horizon, above
the edge of Earth and the wind

pushes it here. The wind
that carries our seeds.

On the table is a loaded gun that has never
been used. It must be used. The air

has turned. Each breath is rotten. Each
could be our last. Every word our last. Our lives
interrupted. Each glass
figurine with tiny brittle limbs caught at the last second
could be our last.

The book is not a survival guide. Nor is it a Bible. Nor is it a hundred and
    one hilarious knock-knock jokes. Nor is it a road map

to California ghost towns. The gun on the table
is pointed at us whether when we're ready and we merely flinch,
or we're not and we buckle.

## Sunspots Disrupt Broadcast Signals for a Week, Driving People Completely Nuts

One woman with a book
and latte, one man with a laptop or a hammer. That's how
these things start. Though they've said it's best

to stay off the streets, nobody's given up
on trying to figure out where people
could meet and fall in love in such a dire time of crisis
and radio silence. What about in surgery? Couldn't a doctor

take a nice look at his or her patient's fat opened heart and say
"there's a place a lot of love could exist?"

That's the sort of clinical fairy tale thinking
that causes people to lean too far off the bridge for a better view
of the beautiful waterfall. Next thing you know,
the great plummet. Imagine

a blue jay flies into a window. Some people would bury it. Others
would desperately try to nurse it
back to health. Sometimes I am in the camp
that would burn the whole house down
to erase the error. If you compact

everything you own into ash,
that makes you worth more than the simple sum of your possessions,
in both gross weight and value.

## What We Can Know from the Footage the News Replays

Six costumers were shot at the mall and the shooter
escaped. The police know nothing
about the shooter. There is an APB and the local
schools are locked down. Every noise outside is amplified. The clairvoyants

will always tell you this train's track

has split in the worst
way, over the deepest
                    ravine. We

are invaded like this all the time. We can't remember
if it's only a recent development or if
these tendrils always wound their way in. Where the walls are weakest.
    The skin

most vulnerable. The brain suggestible. I've had strangers

tell me I smell good. Friends tell me

they like watching me eat.
                    I am in love. I have been

sleeping well. But my lover tells me
I whimper in my sleep. Sad noises she calls them. Little things.

Who is the new gate guard? He looks familiar. He waves everybody by without looking up from his book.

                                        I hear a woman's scream outside

and do not think to call the police. I don't even know
what I'd say. Where it
came from. If it was the television
turned way up in some other apartment after all.

I can't remember faces anymore. Pick anyone
but me from the line

of hostages. Numbers
are our allies. Our resolution is rot.
The witch doctor boils a baby to save the village.

## Accidental Injury and Those Who Are Liable

Early at work in the office building all
of the windows on the thirtieth floor are found shattered
inward. When I hurt

someone inadvertently I want
to be swallowed up by an errant shadow or some other
inexplicable force. Suddenly concern
for my well being. The city grass is killed

by the same chemical in the water designed to keep
our teeth strong. There was only a public outcry

when the hedge animals started to collapse
on themselves. The "check brake fluid" light is on again
you tell me. I am not a mechanic.

There have been

numerous support groups popping up around town for people
with recurring dreams of tornados that lift back up into the clouds
harmlessly just as they are about

to rip a home from its foundations.
And in every reported instance of these dreams

the people are relieved that they have finally gotten a chance to see
a tornado and disappointed when they awake
to find none of it was real.

## Monstrous

To call me tense. Of all people. Take a look
   at the attitudes on the street. People won't even

look you in the eye anymore. We see death
   in every shadow. A thief in every body. And rape . . .

Tense. Ha. The corners of my rooms dip downward.
   They're letting gravity take control, like they

could give out at any second. The sharpest edges
   digging into me, breaking bones, forcing air out.

It's true that I could cause an international incident
   at a moment's notice. No you did not hear pride,

I am here to bring you the truth. Something's
   going to give. Any second. We're all tired

of the wait. It's not pressure. There isn't pressure
   here. There won't be any pressure here. I won't

push you to do something that you don't feel
   is right. You've been wrong, though. When

somebody religious touches my arm it is as though
   they are unclean. A poison burns just under

the skin. I can feel their touch for hours. When
         did our dishonesty turn into something so physical?

Nobody is deluding himself. Me, tense. I want
         people to keep wanting me around for a long

time. Longer than I can even really imagine.
         But also I find I am more and more comfortable

with the idea of no afterlife. Just a great release.
         A defeat. The fear we feel is suddenly loosed

into the air. A terrific rise and scatter. No great
         hand sorting out the terrible sin from the terrible sinner.

I can assure you this isn't all I keep inside of me.

# The Rothko Chapel

As a child, I went on a school trip to a coal mine. The leader flipped out
   the lights to show us what real dark was. In that crushing black, my
   breath pushed its way out of my mouth, as if one wrong move would
   cave everything we couldn't see down on all of us.

I've judged towns by shopping malls and movie theaters. Then by
   store and screen count. Our quick build of neon and parking lot light
   is our monument to the night.

When I've been put under at the hospital, there's a minute when I forget
   who I am, and my thoughts are a severed party balloon. Then animal,
   only animal.

In sleep, who is elevated above the rats who know when the ship is
   burning and when the ship is sinking?

Sometimes mining crews will encounter a rock that can't be picked or
   blown apart by dynamite. And oh, they hammer! Our dreams seep
   into our lives, all loss and impossibility. Every hill isn't scalable. People
   will die to prove that.

Playing racquetball, my retina comes detached. This is something
   internal. I cover my eye, as if this half black could seep outside.

A B-2 stealth bomber is turning above downtown as part of an air show.
   This manmade wing doom, this broken plate of shade, this trap of
   night is raking its shadow across our city's ground. I reach to grab the

door handle, and grip it tight.

A man's shadow mills in front of the window. The latch is undone.

A friend's little brother is playing in a construction dirt pile when it caves in around him. For a week, the town rakes itself apart looking for him. There are dusk vigils. There is newspaper ink.

The city is fascinated by glowing orbs over the local cemetery. News crews are everywhere. Could these be the dead we waited so long to return? And can they forgive us for moving on?

In a nighttime storm I stand outside to watch the wind and I hear the sounds of transformers exploding. The power goes out and the night sky is suddenly brighter than the murk of the ground.

In the movie theater the picture vanishes, and there is a groan that shakes the walls. Even the emergency track lighting seems to lead nowhere.

Why do I always want to cave in and call you when night is trenched and deep, and most people in both our time zones are asleep? I swear I'm not the windmill of saws you left.

The whole room is wired with explosives. There's no telling where the trigger is set.

## Suddenly, a Bottomless Pit

Your girlfriend tells you she's sick of your friends, sick
of your distance and the way you change
the subject every two sentences and your nosy

voice, and it drags you back through all the sadness

you've ever been covered with. Suddenly, you're the mystic
tossed into the legendary bottomless pit. Your books

are twenty feet behind you, their pages rustling
in the dark. We store all our hurt up like miserable panels
under the sun. By the time winter

rolls around, we've forgotten exactly what cold
is like. We think we miss it. We think we're tired
of all the heat summer
has given us. My friend April, a vegetarian,

tells me that over the summer she grilled
up a duck that a coyote had eaten the face off of,
because it was already dead
                                    when she found it. Some days,

a boulder is placed in your path. Others, a suitcase
stuffed with twenties, all leaking out
from the seams. Sometimes it's just
all the socks to the jaw you can recall, and all at once,

because of some words stabbed into your side, between the bones,
where the flesh is weak.

Back in the pit, the wind

roars, and the papers tear. You don't
want death, but you want there to be a bottom.

# The Halifax Explosion

There is such beauty in ruin. The way the ship's bridge burns
        as it lists in the harbor, the drunken steel colossus dizzying
to those gathered on shore to watch the spectacle and gab;
        and the sailors who emerged sogged from the water to warn
of some murderous cargo of buzzing fire and the wiping hand
        of God; and the schoolchildren happy to chuck away math
for half an hour as they speculate lazily at the windows;
        and the burst of white flame that kicks down buildings
for two miles, like poor card houses and wicker tables;
        and the priest's shadow burned into the floor of St. Anne's
Church of the Immaculate, contorted and unsweepable;
        and the anchor thrown five miles inland to lodge heavily
in a small reflecting pool filled with ducks and algae;
        and the porch and nest shattered, the nest the angry wasps
always rebuild after it is knocked down with a broom;
        and sheared girders pressed against the sky at new angles,
a fresh field of hazard for a lost giant's shoeless feet;
        and the windows brushed away like sugar glass as far
off as Truro, leaving shiny wakes on dining room floors;
        and the plume that pours over the harbor, furious and gray;
and the blind ward's new patients with windows pushed
        deep into their skulls, their poor eyes pierced and shredded;
and the sooted rescue workers picking through Haligonian
        dust after weeks of silence because of hope's cruel bug,
the whispered cries of wind rushing past their ear from just
        under this rubble, a girl and faithful dog, or litter of kittens,

or precious photograph, or lovers' skulls, or vague dust, or chum—
    What burn we hold to begin again, and to begin from scratch.

# In Yellowknife, an Inuit Man Is Suspected of Sneaking into Homes at Night and Cutting Out the Organs of People for Food

Already you're in the middle
of nowhere, and in a few moments, night
like a great eyelid. The bushes are suddenly beasts, each stranger

a killer. A gurney pulls
you slowly down an empty street. I've slinked my way
to it, too. I've been ready to take bullet or bat
to the skull, roaming through a dark room
to unknown noise. I've

been to the river with a spear
in my hand. You, too, can let all your lights
burn out, if you do nothing. Eventually,
everything's black. A great eyelid.

The construction vehicles have all collapsed
to the ground, sleeping
giants. The city curfew is enforced by machine-gun
toting cops. The phone
is still silent. The cable's out. Internet
down again. The fridge is filled
with condiments and empty
pickle jars. A knock comes at the door.

## Repossession

My friend needs help but I do not want to help. I am an artist
and I want to be near my art. Around here, that's all
that it ever seems to be about. Wanting. There are posters

advertising A Black Planet, which is just another coffee shop
for moderately successful people to meet and maybe
hook up, whatever, you know. Laura Mulvey suggested

a lot of things that have to do with how we look
at women in movies. That was a third of a century ago,
but still it's sex that sells. Je voudrais death. My friend

called me at three in the morning last night and I did not
answer. I was tired and I knew it would be a long
conversation. My friend said his affairs were all out

of order. Feathers of a shot bird, scattered. My friend, my
friend. I never turn to people when I need them. Films
all over are showcasing the disassembling of women. Every

possible way. You've never seen the way to shake it,
shake it, they say. My friend claims all the books he's ever owned
have had their endings rewritten. He returned home

after a long tour and found the hospital he was born in had been
demolished for a Super Target. These are just
messages, nothing direct. Someone in the apartment above

has fallen. I hear the head hit the floor. When numbers
from area codes I don't recognize appear on my phone
I get nervous. When numbers whose area codes I do recognize

appear, I am excited. If only we were directed,
my friend said once. If only we were all filmed in a way
that made music swell. That made our eyes fill with tears.

## On Our Destroyed Cities

There wasn't ever a real secret buried
under all that rubble. We paid
them to spread that rumor. When they brought

those innocent people
to the gas chamber we changed
the channel. In some far-off cultures,
the losers are the winners. The major interstate junctions

are works of art. Sometimes, when we look up, we think
we see our God. Other times

it's someone else's God. Tube tops
are back in fashion. The new mayoral candidate plays
a twenty-minute guitar solo

on local access. We never stop asking the young girls
when they will be married. And when the next extinction-level event

happens, we have the best cave murals. Our descendants
will know there was never
a scenario we didn't consider in madness.

## Cant

At 1:30 in the morning somebody bangs on your back door. A woman wails outside in the distance. Her sobbing gets closer.

You wake to sirens and the power is out.

On a clear day, one lightning bolt cuts the sky.

Somebody has smashed the window of your car and taken nothing.

The cellar light is busted and there is a groan in the farthest corner.

You have ten unanswered messages from your father and three from your ex-girlfriend on your machine.

Tanks are on the news, slowly rolling down an emptied city street.

The grocery store out of water, gas impossible to find.

The eyes of the dead have been painted over in the old photographs to make them appear living.

Who was that begging at your door? "Please, please, it's so cold, I'm sorry, he meant nothing."

You drive by three black men beating a fourth on the ground. You don't stop.

In the cemetery, grave robbers have struck your father's tomb again.
This time, the body remains unfound.

Picking up the phone to dial, you hear somebody's faint, panicked
breathing.

You pass the body of an old man on the side of the darkest country road.

O, gods of fear! Are we arrogant to believe the world will end in our
lifetimes, as if we in all of history were so important to pull a chair
up to the big exeunt?

Your family left you to face all of this mottled dark alone.

The knives have been removed from the table settings.

Somewhere, A-10 Tank Killers are photographed for a magazine cover.
This is only meant to impress, darling. They are loaded with the most
colorful blanks.

## Chinese Spies

It's not that I don't like people. I want to imagine
a world in which I can give endlessly to others—
my time, my money, whatever it takes. Our voices
would be raised together in celebration, with real
musical tones. In songwriting, the best new melody
is the one that sounds familiar. Please, I just want
to like everybody. Or maybe I just want everybody
to like me. A month ago, I was driving on the coiled
back roads of East Texas, trees relentlessly folding
into more trees, and I had to stop, I had to relieve
myself. There was a shack, sticking out of the woods
not too far from the road, and nothing else for miles.
Two Asian men walked out. There was a stutter
in their step when they saw me and I thought *spies*.
Sent here to gather everything there is to know
about our emptiness. Men in a shack off the side
of State Road Seventeen-Something-Something.
Or in Alaska, perched near a cliff draped in blue ice.
Or my neighbor who sometimes picks up packages
from me that UPS leaves, and always tells me he's
my neighbor, from next door. I want to trust, to give.
I want to be sent away to study all the riveting facets
of solitude, of an American too scared to leave
the phone when it rings at an inconvenient
time. To trust the landscape. A bleak future to embrace.
I know the real idea of generosity is to give especially
when you can't, but that doesn't change anything to me.

The shack. The spies. A neighbor who never knocks.
A familiar harmony without a melody. A stray wind
shuffling down the street. Is this what happens as we
age, our vision of heaven being constantly redefined?
I never thought I'd find the idea of peace so terrifying.

## Unlimited

My finger feels broken. I'm sure I have cancer. I don't
know when the world started
to disintegrate. I don't know the logistics of an A-10
tank killing run. I'm pretty sure I can't cook a soufflé.
It would collapse. It would

                        turn my guests away for good. This is not
the path filled with black cats. This is not
the place the kidnappers said to meet them with
the unmarked bills. Isn't there somebody
                               whose job it is

to call and assure me everything will work out fine? The doctor
was repulsed. He was also incompetent. He said I did not have cancer.
The internet begs to differ

my friend. My personal clutter keeps accruing. It's not interest. It's not
interesting. I'm discarding pieces of paper that I once thought

would save me when the time came.
It turns out the time never came.

It also turns out we're doomed.

                         You know that old song
and dance. The one with all the double basses. They play

the same note for a long time and it seems interminable. The audience
gasps for air when there is suddenly
the dominant.

                    I have been
considering cosmetic surgery. I have been considering
medication for clinical ADD. I just don't have the time
for the test.
          It's two black dots
on a computer screen. This is what we've won

all our wars for. Pharmaceutical satisfaction. I have scaredy-cat pills
for the plane. I have an almost full bottle
                                   of prescription cough syrup.

I have multivitamins. I can't explain to you the details
that make me me. I have a lot of DVDs. I have
some video games. But my game console is now out of date. I have
collectibles. Mainly related to *Star Trek*. I have seven long boxes
of comic books.

I have a real tendency to ramble. I have your daughter.
If you wish to see her alive again you will leave one hundred
thousand dollars in unmarked bills in the trashcan on the corner of . . .

Let me get back to you, she's crying.
Ok, you can have her back. It turns out I got cold feet. It turns out

the lottery ticket was not a winning number. It turns out our children
will never forgive us for our transgressions. It turns out time
is not on our side. It turns out the history books

will not vindicate us. It turns out
there was a lot more we could have done. There still
is. I am not begging you for anything. I have chips. I have clinical
ADD. I have video games and a working air conditioner. We have won

the important wars. I am not a member of the voting public, I am an
alien.

I am inserted digitally.

I don't know when I'm done. I wasn't the one
who told you those things on the phone. I want you

to come and speak to me now. I want your hand on my face. I want you
to tell me there is love in the air
and it is not suffocating us. I want you to tell me our air
is unlimited.
              Our time here never ending.

## The Historic Battleship USS *Alabama*

Floated through bullets strafed by Zeros against her
hull. The kamikaze shower of pilots who were desperate
to prove their mettle for Empire. Now sits in shallow water
for five-dollar tours. No scrap heap, no dismantling. Every old

derelict is loved by someone. You wander through
life, and somebody is sorry
to lose you. My asshole friend's knees

got shredded in Iraq. Catapulted off
the gun turret of a Humvee.
Torn construction paper. Real bloody strips. His wife hovered
over his hospital bed. In town,

she was an ambassador of sadness. A shroud
lowered itself onto her

like spider to prey. When he got better, she left him.
A match is difficult to burn to the end, even if you
can't feel the flame on thumb. Driving into
Mobile, you can trick yourself into seeing the gray outline

of the famous battleship. Really, though, it's hidden behind
a row of storm-tilted trees. What you're seeing are clouds.

## The Things We Own and the Things We Wish to Own

At the gas station before dawn the moths are huge. The size
of dinner plates. Wings
like a paper doll project. Bright colors. Non-
aerodynamic. Gets your heart racing. In a bad way.

So get back in the car already. I told you this wasn't
the sort of place we should stop. There is still

a hum on the air. Something high-pitched. The shadow
of the Earth crept up on us somehow. The radio only plays
gospel stations. Even they're
not coming in clear. Above Atlanta the hills

swallowed the major highways. So suddenly
there were curves and even the small light the stars gave was gone.

A runaway mine cart. The pedals too far
from our feet. And then the hum. It could be power lines

if there were any power lines. It could be cicadas
but the only living thing we've seen are the moths and the gas station
attendant. Sometimes the body

is at home in shade. Other times
it's a razored snare. Reason becomes feathers. When we see
a rest area we will sleep,
O, Charon, O, stream of blood.

## Things We Demand to Know

The local customs. Those we don't know
could be lethal. A misunderstanding and we might be killed
in the worst way.
                          Also, the point of it all.
But that's obvious. Who took the last slice. That's
obvious too.
                  The full extent

of the law—all the little nooks and crannies
in that big old scroll. For instance, if it's true what they say
about the prison term for giving a horse a fedora.

How much time we each have
with those we love. Sometimes we already know that, though.
And still it gets squandered. Like eating the last
slice even though you're not
hungry anymore. It could be saved.
                                    How thick

the pavement is. We've heard ten feet. We've heard
only inches. We've heard a hammer strike to the right point
on a road in Wyoming would cause
a chain reaction that could shatter every road
in America. If that's true.

                  If earthworms
are really used in hot dogs for protein. If we would stop

eating them if that were true.

The exact dimensions of an atom.


If the rumor is true that a scientist looking through an electron
microscope saw a face in an atom. And whose
face that was.


How many strangers have fantasized about us
the evening after passing us. How many friends
have fantasized about us and then felt guilty when we next
met. The weight

of all the paper our names
have been written on.

When the tower topples.


Who gave up our names to the cops. Who
is the real killer. The names of the survivors. Their home
addresses. Their children's home
addresses.

If the people we used to love


think about us and feel pain as we do. If that knowledge
would take some of the poison from our air. If there is a blanket
that could protect us from all suffering.


When the bridge crumbles. The names of the dead. When the heart
   gives out.
The physical one. The one best connected.

# I Am a Wall in a House and I Have a Duty to Remain Erect

*oh Sexual*

I feel as though I am a wall in a house. I have a duty
as that wall. Support. Lately

      I've been thinking of the distance between us. Sometimes
it is a mile and sometimes we are wrapped
in each other. Time can be
                a distance too.
The rooms

         in my apartment are becoming smaller. I know
the paces and the damage that's accrued. The walls
are too familiar. Outside, people are getting furious

in a political way. I thought we were on the same side. I thought our
    foodstuffs
would remain affordable to the general public. I thought
the sound bites would eventually
                end, but instead they are amplified.

I feel as though one strong breath could topple me.

I worry about wrong turns. I worry about these delicate muscles
that move within us to keep us alive. Another
emotional collapse. If I am the wall of a house

then I have a duty to remain erect.
There are a lot of museums in my city. I assure people

49

it is cosmopolitan. But this city has a breath and it is poisonous
to me. I feel compromised. You are so many streets
away from me but I am erect. Hundreds of people live
in my apartment complex alone.

It's the minutia
that takes us apart. Physically. You miss one beat
and you're dead. You take a wrong turn in the wrong
five seconds and it's over. There are wallpaper patterns of doves
and hands releasing the doves. There are wallpaper patterns
of the miracle of highway overpasses. The brain

shuts off during extreme moments of pain or confusion. Petits morts.
   I was never

the wall. My friend said there was a pattern of doves on my wall, but
   he knew
that was not true. There were no doves. There was no voice.

There was an opportunity. There was an endless road.

doves are not
predatory

## A Society in which We Could Be Destroyed at Any Second by Somebody who Grossly Misunderstands Us

We should be honored
that this device has provided
us with so much pleasure. Or was that pressure?

They've been staging the great tragedies
in the public park, free of charge. We don't leave
the glow of the living room. Too much talk,
not enough complimentary gifts. It should be pretty easy

to go through life and never
have a poem written about you, wouldn't you say?

I never forgave you for the pins you snuck
into my shirts. Or
my sheets. We are watching a show on everything
having to do with birds. The murder mystery

was cancelled at the last second. Too bad.

It's nice not to have to learn something, every once
in a while. Somebody tell

those tragic actors to shut up already. We can hear them
right through the walls. Over
our shouting, even.

## You're Invited

To the big show. To a world in which pain
is currency. To a seminar on value. To a seminar
on wealth. To self obsession. To be an outside
dog, with an outside appetite. To perchance.
To make reasonable purchases. To the little
chase. To purr softly. To a room of soft
sounds. To bound suddenly out the door, any
door. To the School of Theatrical Exits. To
not be comfortable with somebody's race,
particularly your own. To the viewing. To swim.
To sink. To throw in everything, etcetera.
To know the words by heart and to learn
the harmony. To hear me. To take the road
leading any which way. To travel, to travel less.
To dance naked in front of the mirror,
you genius. To pull a no-call no-show.
To stand by my side on the firing squad. To know
which one of us has the blank and which one
has the bullet. To blow it all on expensive
cheese and old wine. To participate in the latest
hiring freeze. To wire your best friend some
money, pronto. To live in fear. To take only
according to need. To learn your ability and give
more than you want. To redefine want. To break
the glass underfoot. To take part in real
celebration. To call me more often and sound
like you mean it. To mean it. To wriggle out

of that top. To slide over in the dark. To hum
and drown the spark. To believe me when I say
compassion is not a sign of God. To trust
all roads. To give me all your loss, I can take it.
To understand the language of a breath. Of a hand.
To lean into little deaths. To accept this rhythm.

## Battery and Kinetic

There are street racers in the distance, their angry hum
drifting from downtown. Get me out of here. I know
leave will cure my trembling. I eat and eat. Get me out

of here. I don't know how to store anything up anymore.
Every sound I hear through the walls I accept as threat.
Get me out. The more complex the mind, the greater

the need for simplicity of play. I can't see anything but
façade. Under that, well, you can see where I'm going
murder etc., etc. The one thing we all have in common

is our inability to live without convenience. I expect
to hear a crash when the street racers pass. No, no,
you're right, I mean *want*. Get me? We've been told

that if we willed it, our desires would simply manifest
themselves bloodlessly. The cushion of wealth is one
pin away from deflation. If Death can manifest itself

in one of those classic skeletal hooded numbers, I think
that's how I'd like it all to end, in weary conversation.

## In the Spirit of Forgiveness, I Present the Heartbreak Delegation with a Bushel of Florida Oranges

There wasn't a spot open on the nuclear submarine, so I became
a seventh-grade teacher. I knew
I needed to stop mixing my fantasies
with reality. For some social reason
or other. At a party,

I refused to drink any of the green beer. My rhythm
took hold of me. I danced
in front of many strangers. Some of them threw coins. Others
propositioned me for sex. Some were even
attractive women. A logger

cuts through a redwood he is strapped to, but then realizes
he is strapped to the falling part. Or was that a *Looney Tunes* cartoon?
    There wasn't

a spot open in the local fire brigade, so I criticized
the media's saturation of the word *hero*. In another world,

I could have been mayor of a midsized city in a blue
state. I would pass many ordinances regarding the city's use
of its art funds. Or maybe there wouldn't be any art funds. In that case
I would pass many ordinances regarding the city's use

of its garbage collection funds. There wasn't a spot open
in the line to the sword fighting movie so I got in line

for the depressing movie about human suffering on all corners of our
    planet.
The previews before that one ended
up being much more interesting anyway.

## The Blueprints of the Disastrous Medical Complex Are Hung in the Expensive Museum above Selected Pieces of Bone and Rubble and a Fake Burnt American Flag with the Stars Cleverly Replaced by Dollar Signs

Twenty classic muscle cars in an old barn were found at the bottom of
     Hatchet
Lake. They flooded the land
in the sixties in the name of Bargain Energy. Of course
the soaked cars had no value. But the hi-res
digital pictures won some big photography award. Then the cars
were left there.

                We are sick of our junk. Sick
of it. Like how you never got rid
of the photo albums of dead relatives in the closet. That was decades
ago. Before you were born. You've paid them back
in blood and breath already. You don't need to keep

the messages on your machine. They're mostly silence anyway.
If you have fifty letters from one person that all say "Love This, Love
     That,"
then you can toss forty-nine.

You don't need more than one gun if you have
enough bullets.
                All the old calendars
we kept between the two of us were never
filled with important dates.

A black widow lowers herself
into a box of important files. A tire blowout in the leftmost lane. The

backpack you chose has pots
instead of a parachute. You should have noticed
the weight, though you still fall at the same initial speed.

## All the Evil in the Animal Kingdom

In the heat the glue has melted away and nothing will remain fastened.

Sometimes I still wish it would all suddenly and gently end.

We perhaps could have seen these things coming, if we had looked
close enough.

This body huddling in the corner. This body playing chess, still. This
body glued to the television. Also preserved.

Simultaneously in four continents there is a mass hallucination of a
giant skeletal hand in the night sky.

The bones can no longer hold the skin.

I've been showing a lot of legitimate moments of weakness lately. A lot
of people I know would call that growth.

In nature, a cornered scorpion will sting itself to death, refusing its
enemies the glory of the kill.

So what of repentance.

Love as tree choked in vines. Love as infinite Russian doll. One is
broken in two, and inside there is another. Love as the wrong bottle
from the medicine cabinet.

A pan to catch the blood.

Please call and tell me the story of how everything went wrong again.

In the sixteenth century, a blood-red comet appeared in the night sky
that many thought resembled a figure holding a giant sword for the
attack.

Some blades when heated to almost the point of melting can leave a
wound that nothing will heal, not science, not our best mystics, the
skin white, and the bone burned.

Any notch for any hook will do. Exposed skin. The cheek. The belly.
Furies, oh Furies.

I am still here.

If you look to the night sky, your gaze touches nothing for a million
miles. A dog tumbles into a bottomless pit and starves to death.

There's a real connection here, babe. But I should warn you that I'm not
sure I know what a real connection is.

# Destroyer

I know I lost my girlfriend to your quick pluck
and charm, and soon
you two were married, but now
I understand all of that. I don't wish

the worst highway death and skid of blood on you
anymore. These days I'm impressed
when a new weapon is unveiled, as I am when I see
the guy on the talk show who spins
a hundred plates on sticks. Sometimes, one breaks,
and they all soon follow.

And I'm done with asking the Lord to spare us from
our place in Hell. There is a careful record of the movements made
in our collected name—
this penny means a child starves; this penny means a bullet

passes through a soldier's chest; this penny saves
a village from machete wielding rebels. Our pendulum, our pit,
our precious mayhem. A boy finds a fallen nest of robin's eggs

and chooses not to smash them into a red mess.
A poor young mother can suffocate
her newborn child. Our destroyers wander the oceans.

There are scenarios designed in which their missiles
can be pointed at any city, from Shanghai to Paris

to Lexington, Kentucky. Sometimes,

one plate falls and it doesn't break.
Maybe it is caught at the last second to a great musical
flourish. None of us

think we are evil. Even after
we kick the dog for eating our favorite book, we know justice
is done. And you,
you did what was best for you and the girl, which is all
any of us should be expected to do.

## Terror!!!

There won't be a story. Nobody

would tell it right. At least we can say we know ash. The way
it floats, the way it settles. I feel like a real animal. That gurgle

in the throat. It wants to become a guttural
shout. Nobody would tell the story right. The details

would be muddied up, all distorted. I can look
as cool as anybody with a gun in my hand. With my thumb
on a detonator. I'm talking a real swath
of fire. Oh, just because I admit a fascination with ruin,

I'm the bad guy?

Where do your loyalties lie, anyway?

A group of us all in a dance, animal heat around us, weaving
between us. Dear History,

       I would like a new bike, and a new face.

You know me. You know me,
               you think you know me.

Ha! To have a wave tear us
like construction paper. Ha! To see

a fearful face. American,

you think you are out of the water, but there was never
any land. There will be no land.

I am without a country. Without an idea. Without that new
such and such. My bank account's ceiling
rises every day. Or is that the floor collapsing? I just want to tell you

the story of all the love that's gone wrong
for me. It's a reenactment. I never knew she could be
so cruel. That's part one.
                            Part two is mainly about

heartbeats and the regular circulation of blood. By now
I thought you would have left. You have to appreciate
the way the word "American" sounds yelled
above a panicked crowd.
                            I lit the fuse, but I'll admit
I don't know what it's even connected to. Let's not cut

the line just yet. The silence in here
feels like it could pull us right in. Crush us
together. I never knew how easy it would be to find love in this country

so full of rubble that people don't even notice it.

## Sang

Who is through talking about whom? Who here
has been accused of being full of enterprise?
Incidentally, who here understands every one
of the dimensions of a brick wall collapse?
Who is who, as in which one is which? Who
can save my arm from the fire, quick it's
moving up the wall? Who can spread the salve?
And while I'm on that topic, who possessed
the foresight to bring the salve? Who coveted
the ass, the wife, the wife's ass? Who made
the joke so easy? Who played all the records
when everybody was specifically told they
were collector's items and no longer meant
for human enjoyment? And yes, we danced,
but who cut open their foot on the carpet
nails? Who brought the salve, because that's
for burns and it didn't work like you thought?
Who is meant to save me by singing my
favorite song at just the moment when all
human suffering weighs down on me tonight?
Who can believe it, anyway, all of it swirling
in an awful soup? Who wrought this fence?
Who wrought this misery? Who provides
us the land, and who provides us the till?
Who plots our graves and who lays our heads
down in clay? Who sings melody and who

sings harmony? Who can envelop us in cold
shade, or burn us with the brightest lights?
One breath or something pulling away at us?

## Love in Big City

You're lonely and it's just
now dark. You wish the girl at

the grocery checkout had fallen
into your arms

and told you her worst
secret. You take it, you

take it. On television,
a mobster unloads his

tommy gun into a
cop, and justice

is done. There's that
energy to this place, too.

# Notes

"New Model Honeybee": "O Europe! O ton of honey!" is a quote from the Sylvia Plath poem "Swarm" from *Ariel*.

"Longest Day of the Year": The italicized line is a quote from the Joy Division song "Love Will Tear Us Apart," from the album *Substance*.

"A Guarantee of Protection": The song "All Night Long" appears on the Lionel Ritchie album *Can't Slow Down*.

"Space Phenomenon": The episode of *Star Trek: The Next Generation* referred to is "Remember Me."

"Battery and Kinetic": "The more complex the mind, the greater the need for simplicity of play" is a quote from the *Star Trek* episode "Shore Leave."

## Acknowledgments

Poems in this book appeared in more or less the same form in the
following publications, to which I am extremely grateful:
*Barrelhouse* ("Introducing Love into the Fragile Texas Ecosystem");
*BOMBlog* ("On Our Destroyed Cities"); *Carousel* ("Accidental Injury
and Those Who Are Liable") *Connotation Press* ("Cant," "Longest
Day of the Year," "Terror!!!"); 5 *AM* ("Predatory," "Sang"); *La
Fovea* ("The Blueprints of the Disastrous Medical Complex Are
Hung in the Expensive Museum above Selected Pieces of Bone and
Rubble and a Fake Burnt American Flag with the Stars Cleverly
Replaced by Dollar Signs" and "In the Spirit of Forgiveness,
I Present the Heartbreak Delegation with a Bushel of Florida
Oranges"); *Loaded Bicycle* ("Dementia Unit," "Sunspots Disrupt
Broadcast Signals for a Month, Driving People Completely Nuts");
*/nor* ("Things We Demand to Know"); *Nimrod* ("All the Evil in
the Animal Kingdom," "Destroyer"); *Pinch* ("Battery and Kinetic,"
"Moderate Division Techniques"); *Rattle* ("Chinese Spies," "Feral
Cats"); *Slipstream* ("Suddenly, a Bottomless Pit"); *Subtropics* ("The
Halifax Explosion"); *Washington Square* ("The Rothko Chapel");
*Zone 3 Magazine* ("New Model Honeybee").

Much gratitude to the University of Houston Creative Writing
Program, where many of these poems were written, and to Inprint,
without whose monetary support the writing of this book would
have been impossible.

Many thanks to my mentors and colleagues: Craig Beaven, Erin Belieu, Lauren Berry, Sean Bishop, Matt Boyleston, Andrew Brininstool, Hayan Charara, Darin Ciccotelli, Mark Doty, Farnoosh Fathi, Nick Flynn, Kimiko Hahn, Barbara Hamby, Tony Hoagland, Peter Hyland, Tom Jungerberg, Loren Kwan, Brandon Lamson, Jane Miller, Chris Munde, Brian Nicolet, Paul Otremba, Sophie Rosenblum, Brian Russell, Vanessa Stauffer, Russel Swensen, and Liz Waldner.

Special thanks to my family—Mom, Dad, Michael, Jennifer, Lindsay, and Peter; to Ed Ochester for selecting this manuscript; and to Laurie Ann Cedilnik for moving me always.

# THE MILL ON THE FLOSS

## By George Eliot

A Digireads.com Book
Digireads.com Publishing
16212 Riggs Rd
Stilwell, KS, 66085

The Mill on the Floss
By George Eliot
ISBN: 1-4209-3155-5

Please visit *www.digireads.com*